THE GREAT REMEMBERING

Further thoughts on land, soul, and society

PETER FORBES

THE TRUST FOR PUBLIC LAND
SAN FRANCISCO, CALIFORNIA

Text and photographs copyright © 2001 by Peter Forbes
Foreword copyright © 2001 by Will Rogers

First edition.

Design and production by Ann Aspell, Jenna Dixon, and Helen Whybrow

Cover photo: Dickinson's Reach, Maine
Back cover photo: Grand Gulch, Utah
Frontispiece photo: Meanderlands Farm, Connecticut

The text is set in Fairfield. The display face is Trajan.

Printed in the United States of America

Printed with vegetable-oil based ink on acid-free, recycled-content paper
by Queen City Printers Inc.

Published by the Trust for Public Land
116 New Montgomery Street, San Francisco, CA 94105

All profits from the sale of this book will go
toward the work of land conservation.

Distributed by Chelsea Green Publishing Company
P.O. Box 428, White River Junction, VT 05001

ISBN 0-9672806-1-3

10 9 8 7 6 5 4 3 2 1

This book is dedicated to

Dana Meadows
1941—2001

*who has shown us through the brilliance of her mind,
the fearlessness of her pen,
the strength of her back,
and the wisdom of her heart,
that there is reason to hope
and reason to continue the good work.*

We and our country create one another . . . our land passes in and out of our bodies just as our bodies pass in and out of our land . . . therefore, our culture must be our response to our place. Our culture and our place are images of each other and inseparable from each other, and so neither can be better than the other. In short, what we do to the land, we do to ourselves.

—Wendell Berry

CONTENTS

———

FOREWORD

— —

Will Rogers
PRESIDENT, THE TRUST FOR PUBLIC LAND

The time is right for some hard questions and new approaches to land conservation. Despite recent successes and the growing momentum of national and local land conservation efforts around this country, the pace of development and the impact of often poorly conceived growth on the American landscape have accelerated. Over the next twenty years, we will see the build-out of much of the remaining open land near where people live and work. How do we respond to that challenge? How do we move from a holding action, from "emergency room" reactive land conservation, to a more profound role in protecting our land legacy?

Even as we struggle to set aside more of the special and ordinary places that inspire us, that contribute to our social, ecological, and economic health, and that allow us to feel the touch of nature close to home—even as we strive to do more of what we are already doing—how can we learn to better harness people's powerful connection with the land and the hope that comes from successful place-saving efforts? How can we rethink our work as conservationists to change how our society approaches not just land use, but also our relationship with each other, our sense of community, and our responsibilities as citizens of a rapidly shrinking world? Can the answers to these questions help us create a change in our work that could lead society to embrace a land ethic, reverse the onslaught of the wrong kind of growth, and help all of us better value what we already have?

Peter Forbes has been helping us answer these questions. *The Great Remembering* is another step along his journey from on-the-ground conservation work in New England to a timely exploration of the larger context of land and people conservation. We have invited Peter, as a Fellow of the Trust for Public Land (TPL), to share that journey with us and to explore what lies behind the sense of mission that all of us in the conservation world feel so strongly.

At TPL we have recognized the need to focus more on the *people* in our land-for-people mission. We are learning to tell the stories that show how our relationships with the land—be it an inner-city garden or remote wilderness—help us know who we are and how we can better participate in our communities. That exploration is also taking place in TPL's new Center for Land and People, whose mission is to explore and communicate the benefits of the land and people relationship—from the nuts and bolts to the philosophical. That knowledge is also being developed through our relationship with writers, artists, and other thinkers involved in our Stegner Circle program, as well as through discussions around the country with friends and fellow conservationists.

I have been particularly taken with a model of change developed by the writer, thinker, and activist Joanna Macy, who describes change as requiring three critical elements: a holding action to protect from loss what is already there; a vision for an alternative (and more responsible) system or way of living; and personal transformation to allow us to move toward that preferable alternative.

Many of us in land conservation excel at the first element—protecting what's there. We have helped amass the acres and places to prove it. We fall short with the other two—conceiving and communicating a vision for a society whose values embrace both a healthy land ethic and social equity, and helping ourselves and others find the opportunities to live those values. I believe a measure of our leadership is our ability to demonstrate how land conservation can be an effective entry point for tackling these larger challenges.

The Great Remembering is anything but nostalgic. It takes what our society has forgotten about our relationship with the land and seeks to extract what is most valuable so that we can use it to shape our future. It helps us to realize that our work is as much about helping to build strong communities and personal relationships as it is about saving land. And it shows how we practitioners of land conservation can begin to think about our work as a lever to shift awareness, helping to bring about the kind of profound change that is called for here at the beginning of the 21st century.

The Great Remembering is written for all those whose love of the land leads them to do the hard work of land conservation, but its relevance extends beyond the conservation movement. There are many books, some published by TPL, that explain the technical skills required for the work of land conservation today. This book takes on the harder questions, and asks us to consider how our work in land conservation has the potential to help heal our country and our communities. I believe these are important questions for the Trust for Public Land to ask. I know that others are asking them as well.

I hope you find this book helpful, engaging, and thought provoking. We invite you to join us in this challenge and to share your ideas and thinking.

WHAT IS LAND?

I sit with my feet against the stones of a fire ring deep within Carson National Forest in northern New Mexico. Some ninety years ago, when Aldo Leopold began his career in the Forest Service, he was assigned to this part of the Carson. His travels would likely have taken him to the Vallecitos River and through this same mountain pasture. I look out across shades of green grasses to the gray stone of the mountain and then green, again, reflected in water. Swallows swoop overhead. Sandpipers feed along the edge of the pond and warblers fill the ponderosa. I imagine Aldo Leopold as a young man, shoulders slouched forward slightly from a long day in the saddle, riding slowly across this open meadow. What would have drawn his gaze and his imagination, I wonder. What would he have seen that I can no longer see?

As I sit in this mountain pasture, I recognize that land itself has come to mean many different things to me. In the course of writing this essay, I had grown comfortable using the word *land* to mean soil, trees, nature, plants and animals, even vacant lots, but also as a metaphor for something much larger. Land had come to mean to me both an object and a process. A process, because the point of this essay is to change the way people look at land and their connection to it. Your definition of land, therefore, is as good as mine.

In simplest terms, land is where gravity brings us. Land is where our feet but also our souls and our dreams make contact with the rest of the living world. It is where we feel, taste, breathe in, and smell the more-than-human world. Land is food, ecosystem, and community. Land is life. Leopold wrote "land, then, is not merely soil, it is the fountain of energy flowing through a circuit of soils, plants, and animals." Land, then, is communion. When I speak of land, I mean something closer to "a fountain of energy" than any of its individual elements.

Land is the sweep of one's heart, and the place where we play out our greatest struggles. Like the ancient ponderosa snag that stands before me against the bright blue morning sky, land is slow, ever-changing, and majestic in birth and death. Land is the frothing torrent of milky water that will fill a slot canyon in moments, and it's the green edge of a pond where the water quietly meets the lush marsh grass.

This morning there is a woman in my view of this open pasture. She stands alone with acres and acres of grass around her. Her hands are in her pockets and her legs are soaked with dew as she faces east to be warmed by the early morning sun. *Land is love.*

ONE

THE EXTINCTION OF EXPERIENCE

Even after thirty years, the impression of the place rests somewhere deep inside of me. It rises to the surface on summer days when the color yellow saturates the landscape. In the haze and heat of a New England afternoon, I am transported back to being a child. Suddenly I smell the manure, hay, and dust and remember the row upon row of animal stalls. I cannot look upward without shielding my eyes from the summer glare, and I fear I will lose my father's hand amidst the flowing mass of legs moving past me like so many schools of fish. I remember the time we bought two sheep in the morning and spent most of the day chasing them through the crowds before getting them safely back to the Jeep. My father had been so proud to have struck a deal, and then so embarrassed to lose the animals at the fair. The Hall of Flowers was the single most fantastic thing I could imagine: an entire building in bloom. What I remember most was the moment we passed through the door and were embraced by a hot sweat of sweetness. There were flowers that a

Blue Hill Fair
Penobscot Bay
Maine

young child could only stare at in awe: giant orchids and calla lilies, enormous ferns and orange trees.

Not everything was natural or welcoming about the fair. Much of it frightened me—the crude hawkers standing above everyone trying to shock the passing crowd into entering their sideshows, the chimp that smoked a cigarette while also eating a hotdog and drinking a bottle of Coke, the midget car race with its midget car racers. There were drifters, and pickpockets, and lonely people. I remember meeting a man who was lying in the grass with his head against our car's fender. I talked to him for a while and learned that he "went wherever his hat took him." If not my first experience of fear and pity, it has been my most lasting. As I think back to the annual Danbury State Fair, I see it as an undiluted example of what was good, and bad, and ugly about being human.

And now it does not exist. It hasn't existed for twenty years.

I last attended the fair in 1969, when it had a "Land of the Giants" theme. My mother was volunteering at the state hospital, and a coloring book of the Great Danbury State Fair was given to every child patient. That year, all the fair officials wore bright red jackets and yellow straw hats. Some years later, even though attendance was waning, a petition to save the fair was signed by over 10,000 people.

In 1981, I learned that the fair had closed, and I made a point, driving home from college one weekend, to stop and pay my respects. It was a cold, rainy day, and there was nothing preventing me from driving right onto the parade grounds and walking wherever I wanted. I wanted to see the giant statues of Paul Bunyon and the Pequot Indian, and it saddened me to see how small the statues really were and that they had already deteriorated from neglect and weather. The mountain scenery painted on the high wooden backstops of the parade grounds was badly cracked and faded.

In 1982, the trustees of the Danbury State Fair held a six-day auction that attracted people from all over the country. They sold the fairgrounds to the Wilmorite Corporation for $24 million. Today, the fairgrounds have been replaced with the Danbury Fair Mall, which boasts "world-class shopping 'Connecticut Style' at over 220 stores and shops offering New England's most complete enclosed shopping experience!"

I struggle with this transition, because the fair had such an important and even mythical place in my life. I feel a loss and a concern that the mall—even in its grandeur and style—speaks of a change in my region and my life that somehow diminishes me and those who will come after me. I have asked myself whether I am only being nostalgic for something out of my past. But I am old enough now to have accepted a great deal of change. Why does the loss of the Danbury Fair affect me so? Many will argue that the mall is just a natural extension of the fair, that both were primarily about entertainment and commerce, and that the mall today is as much a meeting ground for people as the fairgrounds ever were. Some could probably even prove, though I would doubt it, that the mall, because of all its modern technologies, has less of an impact on the land than the sprawling ten-day fair ever did. And while these arguments might be true, they miss the point that the fair said more about who I was, who I wanted to be, and who I was afraid of becoming than the mall can ever suggest.

The fairgrounds were where we played out our lives, where our history was recorded. The story of the Danbury State Fair is a history of my region in a changing world. In 1879, the fair was already so popular that a spur rail line was created off the main line heading out to New York. In 1885, one could find forty-five varieties of apples, thirty-one varieties of pears, and fifty-six varieties of grapes being sold there. The schools and factories were closed for a week in 1893 so that virtually everyone in the area could gather together for the fair. In 1896, the first horseless carriage was exhibited on the racetrack. In 1918, an influenza epidemic closed the fair. The fair was reconvened in 1946 for the first time since Pearl Harbor. In 1963, the fair celebrated the life of Walter P. Sweet, a renowned local educator. Ten years later, Leonard Bernstein conducted a Centennial Concert to honor another Connecticut boy, Charles Ives. The fair was a place to see flowers, to buy sheep, to gamble and get drunk, to meet your future wife. What of our history and our hopes is being recorded today at the chain stores and fast-food franchises of the mall?

What makes the Danbury Fair different from the Danbury Fair Mall? Certainly both were places where money traded hands, but the fair had a different motivation than the mall does. The fair was the stage for the idiosyncratic story of our land and our people, and the mall is primarily a place for financial exchange. In replacing the fair with the mall, we have traded a story for the sake of a transaction. This trade, one that we are making every day in almost every place, leads us away from a recorded quirky human history and toward what other writers have called *the extinction of human experience.*

Robert Michael Pyle writes, "and so it goes on and on, the extinction of experience sucking the life from the land, the intimacy from our connections. This is how the passing of otherwise common species from our immediate vicinities can be as significant as the total loss of rarities. People who care conserve, people who don't know don't care. What is the extinction of the condor to a child who has never known a wren?"

On two other occasions in my life, I've returned as an adult to the childhood landscapes that most inspired me, only to find them obliterated.

A dozen times in the summer of 1974, I camped beside a millpond deep in the woods of Connecticut. I can still recall the sense of awe and excitement of coming upon this hidden spot and realizing that human hands had created it perhaps a hundred years before. Giant oaks stood on either side of a stone dam wide enough, perhaps, to drive a mule and wagon across. There was a gentle rise of land overlooking this half-acre pond, and here my friends and I found a spot so special to us that we did what thirteen-year-olds will do: we carved our names in the beech trees and called the place "The Kingdom."

One Thanksgiving twenty years later, I wandered silently for more than an hour through a subdivision, crossing cul-de-sacs back and forth, looking to find my pond. I was sure I was in the right place, but nothing around me looked the same. The stream was gone, the gentle ravine and the dam were gone. When I was about to give up and accept that this was no longer a place but now only a memory, I found myself oriented in just the right way so that even though the land had been transformed by bulldozers beyond recognition, my body remembered. I reconnected with a place that had died. I knew where I was. I looked across a stretch of pavement and saw immediately adjacent to a two-car garage an old beech tree with "The Kingdom" carved in it.

Just a few winters ago, my brother and I took my young daughter to visit the farm where we had grown up. I hadn't been there myself in twenty-eight years, but the place had never lost its grip on me. Some memories from my childhood replay in my mind like images on a filmstrip. In one, I am walking hand in hand with my father, showing him a small stream and waterfall in a patch of forest on the far edge of the farm. He has, no doubt, been there hundreds of times, but he allows it to be my discovery—a private, secret place for me. Quietly, we pick fiddlehead ferns and watercress. He was in his late forties then.

My father had been dead for almost a year when I returned to Bull Run Farm. Though the farmhouse and barns were exactly as I remembered them, the pasture that had drawn my eyes and my feet for so many years had an 8,000-square-foot mansion in the middle of it. Just beyond the barns, in the forest where my father and I had picked fiddleheads, was a twelve-lot subdivision. I walked less than 100 yards from where our sheep once grazed and looked for the stream and the waterfall that had occupied so much of my childhood. I paced back and forth and judged where it should

Bull Run Farm
Housatonic Valley
Connecticut

have been by sighting off the barns. But the stream and the water-fall and even the contour of the land were completely gone.

The woods at Bull Run Farm did not contain any known threatened species of plant or animal, but they did have a profound impact on one little boy's experience of growing up. I was that little boy. Today at Bull Run Farm, there are no deep woods in which a young boy, for the first time, might experience the sense of being part of something bigger than himself. Almost all the smells, sounds, and feel of the woods are gone. As I stood by our old barns holding my two-year-old daughter, Willow, I thought about the possibility of the extinction of real human experience. Maybe new experiences and opportunities had sprung up on this land that now felt so dead to me, but I could only remember how that land had helped me explore, learn, and use my imagination. I realized that what I was witnessing wasn't just the death of a place but the passing of an experience—a gift—that I had been given. I fear what it means for me now that I have only memories and not the places themselves. What will it mean for the children who now live where I grew up, who don't have these natural places? Their experience of life will be materially different from my own. They will lack something. The genes that I inherited from my mother and father may have given me an inclination to roam in the woods, but it was the woods themselves that gave me a sense of independence, beauty, and mystery. My daughter may inherit those same genes, but she will not inherit the experience of that place itself.

Homogenized, sterilized, disoriented, disconnected, rootless. These are the words I fear most for myself and my chosen place in the world. The loss of the fairgrounds and the millpond and the woods where I played and explored as a child and young man makes me ask, How much do I care? How much of my life am I willing to lose? How many farms and waterfalls and forests can we lose before we lose ourselves? How many children will we allow to grow up without the touch of nature close to home? In too many places, this culture of ours has planed away the rough edges to give us a world that has become soft, similar, and unspectacular. When we have little sense of where we are, we also have little sense of who we are. If both land and people lose what is most unique and irreplaceable about themselves, all of us risk being homeless.

CONSERVATION AND CITIZENSHIP

How do I find my own place in the world, given that the physical roots of my life are largely gone? This seems an important question for our times, and I have discovered that many people are asking the same question through their own yearnings for a more fulfilling life in a real place. I have found extraordinary answers in the process and activism of land conservation.

I spent a fall day in 1989 on my knees working the soil in a vacant lot the Trust for Public Land (TPL) had just bought on behalf of a local land trust in South Providence, Rhode Island. For most of the morning, I worked silently alongside a Laotian woman my age. We communicated mostly through laughs and nervous exclamations as a truck barreled too close through the narrow streets or when we found a piece of glass or jagged metal buried in the soil. By afternoon, we had cleared almost a quarter acre and we were comfortable enough with one another for her to try her broken English. Suke was twenty-eight, had arrived with her two daughters just four months before from a refugee camp on the Thai border, and was waiting for her husband to join her. While she waited, she gardened. Every day, she walked two miles through a city she didn't know to a small garden on an almost vacant city block. At the end of our time together, Suke held my hand for a moment and told me that these urban gardens had *made her feel at home in America.*

I cannot think of Suke without comparing her life with my own.

Ebby's Landing
Puget Sound
Washington

She was displaced from her land by a war, and I was displaced from my land by "development." Any time a people's connection to land is severed, whatever the reason, the culture is in trouble. We see stories on television about refugees, and we know there's a problem there. Somehow, we don't see our own alienation from the land and how we have become refugees in our own country. And there was Suke, who was a refugee by political definition, proving her truer citizenship by digging into a new place. Suke knew that she would have a more abundant life when she connected to the land, even in a distant land like America.

In the years since, I have thought often about Suke. I think about her whenever I consider my own rootlessness and am graced by the memory of how quickly she sought land and soil to affirm her place in America. She taught me that home is anywhere; home is a quality of human care and attention. I think about Suke every time TPL completes a conservation project, asking myself, For whom have we conserved this piece of land? Whose life does this touch? How might land conservation change the nature of citizenship?

In 1995 I was in a high school auditorium in Billerica, Massachusetts, in the company of ordinary men and women in an extraordinary time. They were voting to put their community in debt to save a local farm. Griggs Farm was one of the last places in town where one could buy tomato plants in the spring and pumpkins in the fall. The farm wasn't spectacular; in fact, it was sandwiched between two existing malls. But somehow, people knew—even though it wasn't something that could be proved by science— that the destruction of the farm would have meant a great loss of human experience. There was a mystery there, and unexplainable love, that brought people out of their homes to defend the place.

TPL's conservation efforts had given the community a last-minute chance to keep the farm as it had always been, a place to buy locally grown food and to meet neighbors. Developers had plans to build a 300,000-square-foot mall on Gil Griggs's corn

Griggs Farm
Merrimack Valley
Massachusetts

and vegetable fields. There was very little money to do the former, and the promise of great financial reward if the community allowed the latter.

It was a choice of mythic proportions: a small, working-class town already beaten up hard by sprawl taking on Wal-mart developers. These developers were suing TPL and threatening the same action on the community itself. The town meeting had already turned down a request for funds to repair the high school roof, and yet this single act of conservation would cost the community over $1 million. It seemed inevitable who would win that night.

It was a special town meeting, and people were holding their children on their hips while they waited in long lines behind the microphones. They debated the alternatives as if the future of their own families was at stake. They were passionate, and angry, and alive. I heard in their voices the vulnerability and determination of people fully engaged in life. I saw in how they looked at one another their own recognition that caring for the land went hand in hand with caring for their community. For this piece of land, they had left their private lives behind and come into service to a larger world with both great promises and great heartaches. Land conservation had enabled them to realize something greater for their neighbors and themselves. Neighbors were expressing their allegiance to ideals, to one another, and to the land. I understood what this process was enabling them to affirm: citizenship in a specific place. Their decision to go into debt and save Griggs Farm was a form of positive protest, a full expression of their self-determination. They were saying that they could not speak of their obligation to one another without first speaking of their obligation to the land. Their process of building rootedness, through the act of conserving a small farm in the midst of asphalt, was proving that the health of their community would be based on people's sense of service toward one another rather than on the expectation of reward. They were feeling joy and also responsibility, freedom as well as obligation.

David Suzuki, a leading Canadian environmentalist, wrote recently that "consumerism has taken the place of citizenship as the chief way we contribute to the health of our society." While there is plenty of evidence to support this comment, I saw something very different going on in Billerica. I saw people thinking about a healthy future not in terms of what they could do for themselves but in terms of what they could do for others. They were seeing a solution not in terms of economic growth but in terms of relationships. I saw people respond to land in a way that changed them and their community. The act of land conservation offered them the *choice* of place. The act of saving Griggs Farm gave each member of that community something—a place, a belief, a relationship—to share with someone he or she didn't know or otherwise might *never* have been able to know. It was an example, unfolding before my eyes, of how land conservation can tear down the walls that divide people from themselves, from one another, and from nature and become the starting point for a renewed community life.

After ten years working in land conservation, I gradually saw an undeniable pattern emerge—a citizenship of place—that helped explain why some of our conservation efforts were creating changes in people and in the lives of communities that extended well beyond the property lines. In some projects, the act of successfully conserving a place gave people the determination and the tools to make other positive changes in their lives. I saw this happen in cities and rural communities from California to New Mexico to Maine. This change, in a narrow sense, seemed to be really good for land conservation, because the new civic thinking tended to encourage communities to buy and protect even more land. But something else was happening too. More broadly, the first act of conservation was also helping communities address racial tensions, plan more effectively, learn more about one another, strengthen their own local cultures and economies, and figure out what they most wanted for themselves.

In fact, what might have been viewed at first as a social by-product of saving land started to feel to me like a primary motivation. I call this the transformative power of land conservation: how the sense of meaning and self-determination that is brought forward by the act of conservation permeates other aspects of community life. The struggle over land enables people to tackle other struggles. It changes how people choose to live. The essential point of transition is the act of human forbearance. And its greater meaning—what makes conserving land different, in terms of social capital, from building a hospital or a school or preserving an old building—comes from connecting people to nature, connecting people to the wild and the unknown, connecting people to a story greater than themselves.

Conserving a piece of land brings into people's moral universe a renewed sense of fairness, meaning, respect, joy, and love. These are core values that most people share and want, that make most of us feel complete, but that aren't easy to live by today. Many would argue that it's not possible to fully express this body of human values and yearnings without *relationship*, without a deep and abiding connection to the more-than-human world and to one another.

I am very lucky to have met Suke and worked with communities like Billerica so early in my life in land conservation. This brand of "land and people" conservation gave me hope for how we might protect the land community as a whole. I saw a story of redemption, a hope of finding a way for all of us to be at home on the land, no matter where we live or how long we've lived there. These conservation efforts became my benchmark for our work, where the alchemy of human cooperation, activism, and the wild has led people to dwell and imagine differently, to find their own souls.

We all know that another story has been told for a very long time. It's the story of Dr. Suess's Once-ler, who says to the Lorax:

> I meant no harm. I most truly did not.
> But I had to grow bigger. So bigger I got.
> I biggered my factory. I biggered my roads.
> I biggered my wagons. I biggered the loads
> Of the Thneeds I shipped out. I was shipping them forth
> to the South! To the East! To the West! To the North!
> I went right on biggering . . . selling more Thneeds.
> And I biggered my money, which everyone needs.

Fifteen years before *The Lorax* was telling children the sad parable of a forest lost to greed and Thneeds, retail economist Victor Lebow summarized a calling, an American standard of living. In 1955, Lebow wrote, "Our enormously productive economy demands that we make consumption our way of life, that we convert the buying of things and use of goods into rituals, that we seek our spiritual satisfaction, our ego satisfaction, in consumption. We need things consumed, burned up, worn out, replaced, and discarded at an ever increasing rate." This is the story that has created the backdrop and scenery of our modern lives. Popular physicist Brian Swimme tells us that "before a child enters first grade science class, and before entering in any real way into our religious ceremonies, a child will have soaked in thirty thousand advertisements. The time our teenagers spend absorbing ads is more than their total stay in high school."

J. Walker Smith, president of Yankelovich Partners, a market research firm, was quoted in the *New York Times* in 2001 as saying, "In this country, the longstanding solution to getting what you want is to buy something." If we consider the $187 billion the

Paper mill on the Snake River
Columbia Basin
Washington

advertising industry spends on getting Americans to buy things, it is not surprising that we have been tricked into believing that what we want in life is something that can be bought in a store. And the advertisers are breathtakingly successful. While there are now more malls in America than high schools, only 35 percent of Americans choose to vote. Increasingly, we use the credit card, not the ballot box, to place our votes, and the marketplace responds with more aggressive campaigns for our loyalty.

Why talk about consumption and land conservation at the same time?

Our ever-increasing want of things ultimately devours the land while also silencing other stories that may be important for us to hear. This is doubly painful, because in losing our connection to the land we also lose an important source of information about how we might alternatively live. We are left with fewer and fewer sources of meaning for ourselves. I am told that the average person can recognize 1,000 corporate logos but can't recognize ten plants and animals native to his or her local ground. Increasingly, there is only one story to hear and one story to tell. Nowhere is this more obvious and painful than the story of water.

The story of water, like the story of land, is that we have turned it into the stuff of commerce. We used it and abused it, and now we're charging for it. Too rarely are we protecting it. Many of us no longer trust the water that flows from streams or from water fountains or even out of the faucets of our own homes. And with good reason. In 1998, for example, the U.S. Army Corps of Engineers found high bacteria counts throughout the entire Washington, D.C., tap-water system and sharply raised the amount of chlorine in the water. So, we now buy enormous quantities of water. Fifty-four percent of Americans manage to buy $5.2 billion worth of a liquid that just a generation ago was thought to be completely free, clean, and rightfully ours as living beings. Today, we can choose from 700 varieties of bottled water, but we can no longer walk up to a lake or a stream or even a water fountain and drink. Will my generation be the last to once drink freely and healthily of water where it exists naturally in lakes, streams, and aquifers, as opposed to plastic bottles? And what are we saying to our neighbors and relatives who might not be able to afford bottled water? How might our future be different if we spend that $5.2 billion not on bottled water but on protecting water and its movements—the rivers, aquifers, lakes, oceans, and wetlands that are the stuff of life?

Our culture of growth has not, as yet, flourished without the inevitable separation of people and places. The quest for material wealth has definitely kept people working—and that's a good thing—but it has also kept people apart, and that ultimately hurts both land and people. Conservation needs collective action. In opposition to this, industrialism begs for a monoculture: plantations of corn, pines, and people. This is a world where the point of trees is board feet, the point of farms is dollars, and the point of people is to be consumers. In such a culture, everyone begins to worry about getting his or her share, and fewer and fewer worry about doing their part.

Living in the most industrialized and market-oriented society that has ever existed threatens to rob us of our fundamental happiness. If wealth is the surest path to happiness, why isn't our culture already a utopia? Why do so many Americans say that they live with stress, anger, envy, and emptiness? This culture has lifted living standards; lengthened lives; improved nutrition; broadened education and opportunity, and given us equal rights and civil rights. But for many, the pursuit of the American Dream leaves them less than satisfied. Though we definitely get more from this culture in a material sense, it has asked us to settle for something less in a spiritual and emotional sense: less meaning, less hope, less beauty, less good work, less sense of a deep connection to ourselves and to those around us.

Eric Freyfogle, author, lawyer, and educator, sees the resurgence of an American desire to live differently from the way our corporate culture would have it:

> Many worries and hopes lie behind this remarkable welling up of interest in land-centered practices and virtues. The degradation of nature is everywhere a core concern—problems such as pollution, soil loss, resource consumption, and the radical disruption of plant and wildlife populations. Other worries center around food, its nutritional value, safety, freshness, and taste, and around the radical disconnection today, in miles and knowledge, between ordinary people and the sustenance upon which they depend. Then there are the broader anxieties, vaguely understood yet deeply and powerfully felt by many, about declining senses of community, blighted landscapes, the separation of work from leisure, the shoddiness of mass-produced goods, heightened sense of rootlessness and anxiety, the decline of the household economy, the fragmentation of families, neighborhoods, and communities, and the simple lack of fresh air, good exercise and the satisfactions of honest, useful work.

Those who believe that land conservation can build a new commons for land and people have a different story to tell Americans. In this story, we do not surrender fully to a culture defined by self-preservation, the abhorrence of limits, and the expectation of rewards. We create, instead, an expanded parable of land conservation, a story that breathes life into a community-based culture defined by mutual interdependence, a belief in limits, and a love of service. This story doesn't naively suggest that a relationship to land and nature is the whole answer to all our social pathologies, but it offers it as a first answer. Land is the foundation of our cultural house. Our relationship to the land and our

Forest Farm
Penobscot Bay
Maine

ability to listen to its story—one infinitely larger than our own—
are defining choices in who we will become.

The Trappist monk and writer Thomas Merton wrote one rainy
night, "Think of it. All of that speech pouring down, selling nothing, judging nobody . . . what a thing it is to sit absolutely alone, in
the forest, at night, cherished by this wonderful, unintelligible,
perfectly innocent speech, the most comforting speech in the
world, the talk that rain makes by itself all over the ridges.
. . . Nobody started it, nobody is going to stop it. It will take as long
as it wants, this rain. As long as it talks I am going to listen."

TWO

DISSENT AND DEFIANCE

When we take the time to listen, we know what is right and wrong about our relationship with the land. Those who doubt that they are deeply affected by what happens to the land should just drive out to the closest strip development, stand in front, and ask themselves, What does this place say about me? What are we bearing witness to today, and how does this affect our psyche? Nothing speaks more directly to our own condition than what we do to the land. But how do we measure its meaning in our lives?

Harry S Truman was seventy-three years old and in need of a cane when he climbed onto the wooden grandstand and his shaky voice went out over the loudspeakers at the opening of Truman's Corner Shoppers City. It was natural for the businessmen who had created the new shopping center to invite the former president to cut the ribbon, since Truman was still the most popular man in Missouri. What they did not count on was Truman's reaction upon realizing that the shopping center had been built on his old family farm. It was this farm that Truman had referred to years before when he wrote, "I thought maybe by planting corn and getting to know the land I could overcome my shyness and amount to something in life." In 1957, looking out over the new shopping center, Truman said:

> It is a pleasure indeed to be present on an occasion like this. It gives a family rather a bad case of homesickness though. This farm has been in the family nearly 100 years. My grandfather bought it back in 1860. And it's home to all of us. We never spoke of any other place in the United States except this place right here as home. My brother and sister were raised right here. My sister was born here. My brother and I were not. We came here very shortly, though, before we were able to talk and made a home here for our very younger days, and then we've been here on this farm since 1905, as a home residence. My brother and I have planted and plowed corn and wheat and oats all over this acreage here. It's now being turned into this wonderful business center. We certainly hope that it'll be a profitable and successful one, because while we would have liked very much to keep the farm as a home and have used it and run it as a farm, we know very well that progress pays no attention to individuals. We don't want to stand in the way of progress, but that still doesn't keep us from being rather homesick for the places we knew when we were children, places when we were three and five and two years old.

It's unusual to hear someone, especially a president of the United States, expressing human emotion about the land. Truman held his emotions in check, however. "Progress pays no attention to individuals," the former president said as he tried to forget the pain and disorientation he evidently felt. But at the end of his

Sherrod family ranch
Yampa Valley
Colorado

rambling welcome, Truman could no longer contain his true feelings and he pounded his cane on the platform while saying, "And when I get false teeth and get bent over, you'll hear me pounding on the floor and telling the kids what a wonderful place this was before these birds ruined it."

Our emotions tell us, even faster than science does, what is wrong with the picture. Because our emotions are the immediate expressions of our values, they deserve as much attention as does science. Science is the foundation that enables us to express and exercise our skills, awareness, and vital curiosity as humans. We need science because so much of the damage we do is invisible. Science, therefore, enables us to better understand the more-than-human world. Science is critical to expanding our human ethical vision, but it must not replace that vision. It is our human values—not science—that make the initial cry for fairness, meaning, respect, joy, and love.

Can we be brave enough to consider these human values as the highest aspiration for land conservation? What would happen if the whole point of land conservation were to advance values such as fairness, belonging, respect, self-determination, joy, and love? Our training in the biological and earth sciences makes us very uneasy about these questions. How can one quantify meaning? What does one mean by fairness? What's love got to do with land conservation?

A LANGUAGE OF AFFECTION

To use one of Henry David Thoreau's own methods, I will promote the idea that we begin to speak on the topic of land from the heart and from the personal. We have been good scientists. Like Thoreau, let us try to be good poets as well.

I have come to love a small farm that sits above a shallow cove on Penobscot Bay. I don't own this piece of land, but I walk its perimeter with Walt Whitman in mind when he wrote, "the press of my foot to this earth springs a hundred affections." I feel in my bones that there's a much larger story here than I might ever fully know. Just down the dirt road from this farm are high, rocky blueberry barrens that span both sides of the road and afford everyone a spectacular view out across the islands of Penobscot Bay. I've walked across those barrens dozens of times enjoying the view, the sun, the fog, and more often than not a few handfuls of berries.

I heard a story last summer that brought me back to my favorite blueberry barrens. A woman from The Nature Conservancy had been asked to visit a local town and tell the residents what she found to be "important" about the land in their community. She came to realize, by their choice of the word *important,* that the townspeople wanted her to find land with rare and endangered species, land *worthy* of protection. But she also knew from her visit that what the people of this town really *loved* were the blueberry barrens. They hiked them in summer, picnicked on them in fall, and enjoyed the view across them every day of the year. There probably wasn't a single person in that community who didn't know those hills or have a personal story about that high, exposed stretch of land. And certainly, at one time or another, everyone had enjoyed eating berries from those barrens. The nutrients that gave life to their passions came from the land under their own feet. Those blueberry barrens enabled those people to be *of that place.* Why is it, then, that they needed someone else to tell them that they could protect what they loved? Why is it that they needed the excuse of its being home to an endangered species to protect it? How do we measure, or even explain, what is important if it isn't about other species? These people saw the loss of those barrens as endangering something in themselves and in the vitality of their community, but they didn't know that such feelings were enough to act on.

In many different cultures, a vital human relationship to the natural world is expressed directly in the volume and diversity of language. Barry Lopez has shown us that the Hispano culture of New Mexico uses the word *querencia* to mean affection or longing, and in common usage it means one's sense of responsibility toward a familiar place. In native Hawaiian, the words for *family* and *community* are both related to the plant taro, which was once the staple food.

The Hebrew word *shalom,* which can mean both hello and good-bye and which literally means peace, has its root in the words *complete* and *whole.* This makes sense. It feels correct that to be at peace one must experience completeness, to have nothing missing. What are we missing today? What do we most want as human beings?

In our European culture, we have hundreds of technical, scientific terms to explain the habitat needs of most plants and animals. It is a great accomplishment of our civilization that we can study any particular wetland and relatively quickly assign to it a whole value system that will, in many cases, enable us to protect the very things we say we value. The existence of words such as *endangered species, ecosystem,* and *habitat* demonstrates that we have a science of preservation and a commitment to a diversity of species.

Furthermore, this science has led to laws such as the Endangered Species Act, which codify and enforce a set of values that our governing system says are held by a political majority. Why is it, though, that we have so few words to describe the shades of love that most farmers feel for their land? Why is it that we have so few words to describe our land ethic? Why is it that we have so few words to describe the love that a biologist feels for his or her subject matter in the natural world?

In one important sense, the existence of natural science, its technical jargon, and the laws it has helped pass are collectively an expression of respect, if not love, for the land and all the life it supports. Although these words may move laws and regulations, they are not words that move people. Through our language, we make our relationship to land and nature so abstract and distant

Levi Holt, storyteller
Nez Perce Nation
Idaho

from our own human experience that it becomes bland. We become so helplessly tongue-tied that we cannot adequately express even our simple love for a blueberry barren. Do we lack a language of true affection for the land, or do we lack the affection itself? We respect science over emotion, reason over feeling, and so we conclude that affection is not enough.

Wendell Berry writes in *Life Is a Miracle* that "the language we use to speak of the world and its creatures, including ourselves, has gained a certain analytical power (along with a lot of expertise pomp) but has lost much of its power to designate what is being analyzed or to convey any respect or care or affection or devotion to it. As a result, we have lots of genuinely concerned people calling upon us to 'save' the world which their language simultaneously reduces to an assemblage of perfectly featureless and dispirited 'ecosystems,' 'organisms,' 'environments,' 'mechanisms,' and the like."

We can't hope to change culture without first changing how people talk. The civil rights and equal rights movements figured this out. In order to evolve beyond a *technical* movement capable of changing laws into a *cultural* movement capable of changing how people lived and acted, they had to evolve the words we used. For example, *Negro* became *black* became *African American*. *Mankind* became *humankind*. The lack of language to adequately express our love of the land is the clearest indication that, despite our enormous successes in saving land across the country, we are losing the battle for the soul of America.

If we can work and talk not in terms of dollars raised and acres saved but in terms of human lives transformed, our projects will, indeed, become parables for another way to live on this earth. At the core of this evolution in the history of our movement is language itself. Berry writes, "We know enough of our own history by now to be aware that people exploit what they merely have concluded to be of value, but they defend what they love."

How true. My friends in Maine did try to defend what they

loved, but those who wanted to exploit its value got there first. On my last visit, an 8,000-square-foot mansion stood right at the height of land in the middle of the beloved blueberry barrens on Penobscot Bay. The townspeople talk of sorrow for what has been lost, and they wonder what the owner was thinking. But what were *we* thinking? We didn't have the words to express our love or the ability to convert that love into action.

THE ETHICS OF ENOUGH

When giving talks, Thoreau often asked of his audience, "Let us consider the way in which we spend our lives." You do not have to be a scholar of the man to know that Thoreau's insistence on self-determination and individuality was central to who he was. He refused to be homogenized, to march in step, to live outside of his beliefs. Over 150 years ago, he was pointing out the ills of society and the pressures to conform and noting how these things were tampering with the land and with our ability to lead meaningful lives. So what I am saying about disconnection and alienation is nothing new. It is something very old. But the societal pressures Thoreau wrote about have only grown more extreme, and the voices and examples of how to live differently or to act out against the homogenization of our world are less available. Today, it is appropriate to consider the act of land conservation as a form of civil disobedience that quietly but steadfastly opposes the prevailing cultural forces of our times. Our determination to protect—and to recreate when necessary—the places we love the most calls on us to make sacrifices, to express our dissent and our hopes in ways that many of us have never done before.

Aldo Leopold envisioned all this. Writing more than fifty years ago, he said, "conservation is one of the squirmings which foreshadow this act of self-liberation." Let us begin to think of land conservation, then, truly as an act of self-liberation—liberation

Abandoned fairgrounds
White Mountain foothills
New Hampshire

from ways of living that deny us meaning, purpose, and joy. Conservation is self-determination, choice, and the highly visible expression of our own *ethics of enough*.

Leopold gave us the phrase "a land ethic," and his ideal strikes me as even more unrealized today than when he first spoke of it. An ethic for land is more abstract to people in 2001 than it was in 1949. There is, however, a growing sense of an ethic of enough. Enough trying to keep up with the Joneses; enough loss of our favorite places; enough loss of different forms of life; enough traffic; enough pollution of our food, air, and water; enough waste. There's no more potent talisman of this condition than the announcement in 2001 that the Fish Kills dump in New Jersey had become the largest man-made structure in the world.

I am optimistic that, as a culture, we have not yet completely chosen how we want to live. The case is not yet closed. We've surely sampled the feast and find it hard to get up from the table, but there's lots of evidence that many Americans are seeking alternatives. For example, in the 2000 national elections, Americans were split over who should be president but united in their choice to support land conservation across the country. In 209 referenda in thirty states, 83 percent of the time the majority of voters said yes to putting themselves in debt in order to acquire and protect more public land. In places as diverse as Broward County, Florida, St. Louis, Missouri, Gallatin County, Montana, Gwinnett County, Georgia, and Seattle, Washington, average Americans expressed a resounding ethic of enough through both their ballots and their wallets.

Thousands of conservation projects around the country provide evidence of the emergence of a different expression of the soul of this country, and it is an expression of love and self-restraint rather than apathy and self-interest. In Bill McKibben's powerful essay "How Much Is Enough?" he asks us to consider different ways to judge the success of our culture. To those who believe that constant growth is what counts most, success might be measured by all the various ways we have exhibited our power and control over the world: from the telescope to the steam engine to the airplane to nanotechnology. If we can view our culture, instead, as a maturing individual, we might choose other things as our defining moments: actions inspired by humility, compassion, restraint, and wise leadership. McKibben writes, "My point is only that the seeds of other worldviews exist within our present culture. To follow them would require that we act on the one uniquely human gift: our capability for self-restraint. As birds have flight, so this seems our special glory."

The act of conservation is an act of forbearance, of restraint. Through this special relationship with the land, we come to understand patience, interdependence, diligence, and respect. We learn a sense of limitations. Through land restoration, we come to see how humans can restore habitats and make amends. Perhaps most important, in a world hell-bent to demystify, explain, and control, a relationship to the land is a way of remystifying one's life. In receiving mystery back into our lives, we are accepting our inability to have all the answers and control all outcomes. Can we really know all the answers? This place of unknowing is fertile ground for developing sympathy with the rest of the living world. With all the pain and suffering that continues in this world, it seems that an essential characteristic of being human is the capacity for empathy and bearing witness to that which we cannot control. An aeronautical engineer who began practicing Zen in the late fifties, Roshi Bernie Glassman, says, "when we are ready to live a life without fixed ideas or answers, then we are ready to bear witness to every situation no matter how difficult, impossible or painful it is. Out of that process of bearing witness—healing action spontaneously arises."

Glacial Lake Camp
The High Sierra
California

TPL's efforts to save Griggs Farm in Billerica had another power-ful impact on my view of land conservation. TPL eventually won the lawsuit that followed the community's vote. In addition to $2 million to protect the farm itself, hundreds of thousands of dol-lars in staff time and legal costs were required to fulfill the will of the people of Billerica to see Griggs Farm remain a farm. We were victorious, but at a huge cost. Late one night, I read our oppo-nent's annual report and learned that they had spent $587 million that same year buying other farms and forests for new develop-ment sites. This sum is equal to almost *half of all the money avail-able* at all levels of this nation's public and private sectors to con-serve land. While we "won" in Billerica, a tidal wave of epic proportions had crashed over us, swept more places away, and we didn't even know it.

It does no good to keep our heads in the sand. We celebrated a victory at Griggs Farm, but during that same hour, three other farms were converted into malls somewhere in America. The American countryside is being transformed by sprawl at 365 acres per hour. Our own federal government tells us that almost 3 mil-lion acres of forests, farms, and open spaces will be developed this year. Hardly a single place in our country will be spared. New Hampshire is being developed at a rate of 15,000 acres a year. Maricopa County in Arizona loses seventeen acres of pristine desert to development every twenty-four hours. Atlanta's growth pressures cause clear-cutting at the rate of thirty acres each day, giving Atlanta the distinction of consuming land faster than any settlement in human history. California—already the world's sev-enth largest economy—is still growing, to the detriment of one of America's largest concentrations of endangered plants and ani-mals. Americans living in the West have watched their beloved mountain backdrops—the Boise foothills, the Rockies, the

Wasatch Range, the Sangre de Cristo Mountains—all be developed at levels unprecedented in our land-use history.

We are humbled by our small steps, yet of course, we must still take them. What we can do may be small, but still we must do it. We cannot afford, however, to remain confused or conflicted about *why* we do what we do. Griggs Farm taught me that the act of land conservation is too often focused on treating symptoms as opposed to addressing the root of the problem. The crisis of losing a beloved forest to strip development is similar to the crisis of a human being suffering a heart attack. Prevention is better than radical surgery. The long-term cure for the loss of wilderness is not merely buying and protecting some wildlands but rebuilding a culture of sympathy for and reliance on the land, just as the complete prevention for another heart attack isn't bypass surgery but changing the patient's way of life. Certainly we must use the technology of saving land and performing heart surgery as much as we can, but we must try equally hard to prevent the problems in the first place.

It is fundamental to the ultimate success of land conservation that our work changes not only public life but private life as well. Fighting the loss of wilderness, regreening our cities, saving endangered species, controlling growth and sprawl, and protecting special places are all critical, but they may not be significantly addressing the source of the problem. And the source of the problem is how we humans live each day. There are no environmental problems that don't start as people problems.

David Orr has given us this analogy: Imagine a bathroom with an overflowing sink at one end and a mop and bucket at the other. The technological solution is to use the mop and bucket to clean up the spilled water. The ecological solution is to turn off the water faucet. Trying to solve our environmental problems by conserving land or passing laws is a great technological solution, but we are failing to keep the bathroom floor dry. The ecological solution is to rethink land conservation as the conservation of culture.

Lake Tarleton
White Mountains
New Hampshire

When Aldo Leopold was formulating his seminal thinking about ethics and the land, he wrote to his friend Doug Wade, who was a naturalist at Dartmouth College, and said, "Nothing can be done without creating a new kind of people." This idea would emerge five years later as the strong theme of *A Sand County Almanac,* where Leopold was even more emphatic that the purpose of land conservation is to teach about right and wrong living. "Conservation," wrote Leopold, is defined by "a state of harmony between men and nature," which assumes shared values between the two. Leopold was nervous about a form of conservation that is valueless, that "defines no right or wrong, assigns no obligation, calls for no sacrifice, implies no change in the philosophy of values." He saw conservation as a moral argument that might create a healthier, whole-land community that includes people. In this light, the point of land conservation is less about recreation and more about human re-creation. Imagine, for a moment, that the purpose of land conservation is to help *create a new kind of people.*

Since Leopold wrote *A Sand County Almanac* calling for an American land ethic, the number of environmental laws and organizations has grown one hundredfold at least, and the emergent study of ecology has led to a whole discipline for the protection of endangered species called conservation biology. Our laws have changed a great deal, but to what degree have our daily lives? Since Leopold was really speaking to the private landowner about land ethics, it's valuable to look at what has happened to private land conservation as one evidence of change.

There are now 1,250 private, nonprofit land trusts working at the local and regional levels in America. This does not include the extensive conservation work conducted by national organizations such as the Trust for Public Land and The Nature Conservancy. Local land trusts have tripled in number since 1980, and now over a million Americans contribute to local land conservation. By comparison, there are 700,000 members of the Sierra Club. By 1998, land trusts had conserved 4.7 million acres of land, which was a 135 percent increase over the decade before. By and large, these are local organizations run mostly by volunteers or small staffs. They were born more often than not from a local story of love and loss between land and people. And they have come to reflect the diversity of the local landscape. TPL has helped create a land trust in Hawaii that protects taro fields and teaches about Hawaiian culture, a trust in the Bay Area that promotes local agriculture, a trust in the Bronx that grows food and good neighbors in urban gardens, and a trust in Maine that perpetuates the lifework of Helen and Scott Nearing. Land trusts have a wealth of stories and metaphors about how we might live alternatively, each unique to its region. More than national organizations, it is land trusts that are communicating directly with people and participating in decisions about their lives. Choices between right and wrong living, and the restraint required to protect what one loves the most, are played out every day as growth and change put pressures on the land. But very few land trusts talk about ethics, values, and ways of being human.

When asked today to state their primary reasons for saving land, most conservation organizations have no clear philosophy beyond the critical motivation of preserving biodiversity. One might hear explanations ranging from community development to local self-reliance to viewshed protection to wilderness protection to stewardship to ecopsychology, but we have no guiding principles and no language to gather up these valid explanations into something that resembles a well-articulated philosophy or practice. Those conservation organizations devoted to preserving the earth's endangered species have, through conservation biology, a clear set of objectives covering how and why they do their work. There is nothing comparable to guide the majority of conservation organizations that are interested in protecting a way of life that includes biodiversity, growing healthy food, safe parks and clean rivers, a culture of mutual aid and an appreciation of local beauty, a vital cultural history, and local sacred places—all of

La Perla Community Garden
Manhattan Island
New York

which contribute immeasurably to the human experience. The Land Trust Alliance, the trade organization for land trusts, has a well-formed set of standards and practices for *how* land trusts should conduct their work but is silent on *why* they should be saving land.

Land trusts and land conservation have been a true success story. But now they have reached the tipping point, where they are poised to have a significantly larger impact on society based on the choices they make today about their own purpose. The contemporary conservation movement, born in the 1970s, has proved its technological prowess. It has won important political victories, passed many laws, shaped government, competed successfully for land, and changed the nature of land tenure in America. Millions of acres of land have been saved. Can conservationists now turn with equal strength and tenacity to influencing private life? Can we grow from a technical movement into a social movement?

The Artic National Wildlife Refuge (ANWR) is a perfect example of why this transition is so essential. Conservationists view the ANWR as a great achievement of humanity. We have set aside one of the last remaining intact ecosystems in our country in what is ultimately a moral response to what is there. Through the act of conservation, our relationship to that place is defined forever by forbearance, and we are ennobled as a result. But what happens to us if we trade this moral response for an economic one? If our relationship with that part of wild Alaska can be changed to one of utility—if the ANWR can be opened to oil extraction—then we are significantly diminished as a people because we could not honor that relationship. When we view conservation in terms of relationship, it is clear how the work of conservation is the struggle for the soul of America.

I spent five months of 1999 living in and observing a dozen communities—from ranching communities to Indian reservations to wealthy, sprawling suburbs—to see what I could learn. And I learned a great deal about the core questions that move me and challenge me about our work. These are the questions that I believe we *cannot* avoid: In service of *what* are we saving land? Can we succeed in saving land without also helping people choose how they want to live? What does success look like?

Thankfully, there are many examples of how land conservation is touching human lives and transforming communities. The best of these are not "projects" in the conventional sense but parables for another way to live. Classie Parker organized her neighbors in central Harlem to take better care of one another by creating community gardens in vacant lots. Glenn and Kathy Davis are learning Hawaiian traditions and rebuilding native culture by bringing young Hawaiians back to the taro fields. The ranching community in Yampa Valley, Colorado, is maintaining both natural diversity and a deeply rooted way of life by conserving ranchlands. Miguel Chavez is trying to heal the deep ethnic divisions in his native Santa Fe by creating a new downtown park and farmers' market. Richard Skorman became a political leader in Colorado Springs because of his and his neighbors' commitment to finding and expressing their own ethic of enough. In each case, the act of saving land created new potentials for these individuals and showed the social promise behind a reconnection to the land. These stories challenge us to think and speak differently about the work of land conservation; they also promise us that our work can have much greater impact than it has had to date.

Somehow, we must add to conservation's great technical achievements the ability to persuasively and humbly make moral arguments. In saving land, we must learn to speak a language that engages and challenges the heart and soul of our neighbors. By listening and showing our awareness of what's happening around us, we can begin to boldly search out a way to change our culture, just as we have searched out a way to change our use of the land. As a conservationist, I used to wrestle with what Bertolt Brecht meant when he wrote, "unhappy the land that requires heroes." I had always thought just the opposite and rather liked the idea of being

Homesteader's desk
Machias Bay
Maine

a hero, riding into town on a white horse to save the day *and* the land. Being a hero, quite frankly, has always been good for land conservation's image, but I recognize now how heroism without clear and compelling moral arguments might actually be hurting the land. We must not under any circumstances abdicate our personal responsibility to live with care, even by making a contribution to an organization that might claim to do that work for us.

Land trusts and conservation organizations, in general, now have a higher calling, a higher responsibility, than they had in the past. The problems we face are not technical or political or even environmental; they are moral. And though we must reply with all our best technical means—the saving of land and the passing of laws—we can't forget that the only viable response to a moral problem is a moral approach. Leopold told us this in his essay "Ecological Conscience":

> We have not asked the citizen to assume any real responsibility. We have told him that if he will vote right, obey the law, join some organizations, and practice what conservation is profitable on his own land, that everything will be lovely; the government will do the rest. This formula is too easy to accomplish anything worthwhile. It calls for no effort or sacrifice, no change in philosophy or values. It entails little that any decent and intelligent person would have done of his own accord. No important change in human conduct is ever accomplished without an internal change in our intellectual emphases, our loyalties, our affections and convictions. The proof that conservation has not yet touched these foundations of conduct lies in the fact that philosophy, ethics and religion have not yet heard of it.

Thomas Godfrey, who lives on a beautiful island in Penobscot Bay, summed up this situation when he expressed his thoughts about working with his family and a land trust to protect his own beloved piece of earth: "I hate giving in to the necessity of taking this step in the first place. To put a conservation easement on these islands should be unnecessary. To protect such a place is to admit that it is in danger and that, in many ways, the human race is out of control." Godfrey and his family did protect their land by collaborating with a land trust, and that is an important statement about land trusts as keepers of faith. We live in a society defined by laws—prohibitions—more than loves. In a world without a moral bottom line about how we should treat the earth, how we should live, we can only rely on laws that define what we can't do. What, then, tells us what we should do? The answer: an evolved and shared sense of love; a shared sense of an evolving and maturing relationship with the land.

THREE

BUILDING A NEW COMMONS

C lassie Parker lives in Harlem just a few blocks from the hospital where she was born. For many years, Classie felt stuck on a street where no one knew anyone else and drug dealers ran everything. She especially feared for her father, who was growing old and needed a way to stay active and get outside. She worried that he would die alone in a building where nobody cared. In 1992, Classie's apartment stood adjacent to a 3,600-square-foot vacant lot that was crowded with crack vials, needles, abandoned cars, and garbage of every kind. When Classie got the idea to create a garden on that lot for her father to work in, she recruited her brother and a Hispanic couple who lived nearby and their five children to help her. Classie had a vision for a place where the old and young could work together. Today, the thriving garden there is called "Five Star," in honor of the five adults and five children who started it.

One very hot Saturday in July, I found myself on 121st Street in Central Harlem trying to get perspective. For an hour or more I sat on the corner of Frederick Douglass Avenue eating peaches and

Classie Parker in Five Star Garden
Manhattan Island
New York

taking in the neighborhood. There was constant motion everywhere: motorcycles racing each other down the avenue, vendors selling sunglasses and old record albums, children playing games at my feet, endless flows of people. What I really wanted was a view, and I eventually met someone who had one to offer.

She unlocked the door of her building, held it open for me, and casually told me how to find my way to the roof. When the heavy metal door slammed shut behind me I had to stop short to let my eyes adjust to the near complete darkness inside. The hall had no lights and the street level windows were blacked out. A long shaft of light from a second floor window lit a set of wooden stairs, which was strewn with clothes and cigarette butts. The air was still, cool, and musty. As I climbed the stairs I passed rooms with their doors set ajar and heard voices inside. Through one open door, I glimpsed a man whom I had seen earlier, then elegantly dressed and now sitting on a single mattress on the floor, his shirt off, his head in his hands. As I made my way through the hallways and up the stairs no one seemed to notice me, even the two children who ran out from the darkness and across my path.

When I reached the fourth floor and pushed open the door onto the roof, the motorcycles, boom boxes, metal, and heat of the city grabbed me instantly and I squinted in the glare. But amid all the noise and pavement and broken glass, there below me was a quiet green garden. An eight-foot-high chain-link fence could barely keep the sunflowers from pouring out into 121st Street. With two large townhouses protecting either flank, the garden itself was just plain bold and beautiful. A dozen discarded lawn chairs had been retrieved and organized loosely around leaning tables and empty crates as if a card game or a good meal had just been finished. I could see rows of corn, plots of vegetables, climbing snap peas, grapevines, fruit trees, and a dogwood. I could hear birds. Men and women of all ages were hanging on the chain-link fence talking to friends on the street, and then quickly turning back into the garden with a hoe or a laugh.

Five Star is breathtakingly beautiful and heavy with life. It is stewardship and wildness wrapped together and dropped down on 121st Street. Classie produces food, beauty, tolerance, neighborliness, and a relationship to land for people throughout her part of Harlem, all on less than one-quarter of an acre. Five Star Garden is almost absurdly small, but for the people of 121st Street—who, for the most part, never leave Harlem—the garden is their own piece of land to which they have developed a very deep personal attachment. These are Classie's words:

> Once I started working with the earth, the love in people started coming out. People I didn't even know, strangers literally would come in and say, "Oh, I love this." And they started telling me their life stories . . . where they came from, how old they were when they first started. They were telling me things that they didn't even tell their own people. So it was like a healing for them, too. When they left they seemed changed. One was the lady with Alzheimer's. She and her aide were walking by one day and they saw the garden so they decided to come in. We didn't know she had Alzheimer's but the aide knew. And within thirty days the lady made a complete change. When she first came the lady seemed listless, like living in her own world. And the other seniors started talking to her; acting like it was a natural thing. And pretty soon she started talking back to them. This lady, come to find out, was a dancer with the burlesque dancers back in the 1930s and she got up and she showed us how she used to kick her leg and tell us about all the pretty things she was wearing. One night, this lady's son came and only Daddy was here at the garden. And he said, "I just come to see if this thing . . . if this garden is real. Because I cannot believe the change that has occurred in my mother."

We think of ourselves as farmers, city farmers. Never environmentalists. We love plants, we love being with the earth, working with the earth. But there is something here in this garden for everyone. And any race, creed, or color . . . now, can you explain that? This is one of the few places in Harlem where they can be free to be themselves. It's hard to put into words what moves people to come in this garden and tell us their life stories, but it happens every day. There's love here. People gonna go where they feel the flow of love. There is a difference. You come in here and sit down, don't you feel comfortable with us? Don't you feel you're free to be you? That we're not going to judge you because you're a different color or because you're a male? Do you feel happy here? Do you feel intimidated? Don't you feel like my dad's your dad?

Even Classie Parker admits that there is a certain mystery as to how this garden thrives so successfully among the noise, cars, motorcycles, and concentration of human life. Any effort at reductionism fails. But what is clear is that Classie acts and speaks from a natural language of affection. Her effusive love of the garden and the neighborhood is infectious. When she describes her work and her life, she tends to speak of emotions and values. She uses easily understood words like *love, neighborhood, earth, hard work, joy, fear*. She is not an environmentalist attempting a specific program with established goals and procedures. She is an African American living in Harlem who is growing food because she loves to, because she cannot *not* do it. Her love breeds courage and an integrated way of thinking. She believes fiercely in the local integrity of her work but simultaneously connects it to a larger story. By finding her own authentic place in the local web of life, she feels a responsibility to create

Five Star Garden
Manhattan Island
New York

change within larger communities. It's as if one kind of citizenship inspires and obligates another expression of citizenship. Lastly, as a final grace note, others who come into contact with this garden yearn for what these lives and relationships have to teach them. A small group's simple work, and the change that their work creates, makes them leaders. Their stories are parables of another way of being human on this planet.

What can conservationists learn from Classie Parker and Five Star Garden? At The Trust for Public Land, we ask ourselves what connects acts of conservation at a place like Five Star Garden in central Harlem with a landscape like the Columbia River Gorge in Oregon and Washington. The gorge is a large, majestic ecosystem, home to a great diversity of species, and it offers humans a physical experience, a potent reminder of the inspirational power of wildness to nurture the body and soul. If we define conservation success in terms of acres, the distinctions between the two are obvious and enormous. If we are committed solely to biological diversity, the gorge has something very important to offer while Five Star Garden does not. If we enjoy the debates between wilderness and stewardship, there's an argument for both the gorge and Five Star Garden. And if we are interested in sociology, Five Star Garden is the perfect example of a human relationship to land that is transforming a community. And yet all these explanations and ways of defining success are ultimately inadequate for the future of land conservation. None examines the whole of life, and therefore each perpetuates an unstable system. We must instead strive toward a new radical center where the tiniest urban lot and the largest tract of wilderness are viewed through the lens of a new objective, a new aspiration for land conservation. As Thoreau put it, "new earths, new themes demand us!" The theme for this new aspiration for land conservation is *relationship*.

BUILDING A NEW COMMONS | 55

If we wait for science to give us all the answers, we will always be too late. The radical center of land conservation demands that we combine science, human intuition and values, and a commitment to what it takes to live in a whole-land community. Writing in 1935, Leopold asserted that a great deal of our inability to gain consensus on what is right versus wrong living comes from the physical and intellectual separation of the human and non-human worlds. He wrote:

> One of the anomalies of modern ecology is that it is the creation of two groups, each of which seems barely aware of the existence of the other. The one studies the human community almost as if it was a separate entity, and calls its findings sociology, economics, and history. The other studies the plant and animal communities, and uniformly relegates the hodge-podge of politics to "the liberal arts." . . . The inevitable fusion of these two lines of thought will, perhaps, constitute the outstanding advance of the present century.

If the first step in achieving Leopold's aspiration has been the creation of conservation biology, then the second step might be something called conservation sociology. The first is the application of the biological sciences to guide the process and purpose of saving land. The second would be the application of social and ethical considerations to guide our reasons for saving land. The fusion of both could then become the new radical center for land conservation. Our land and our selves beg us to create that fusion. This isn't saving land *without* people. And this isn't saving land *for* people. The fusion that Leopold called for is saving land *and* people. The challenge for land conservation is to create a cycle of nutrients and benefits that flow uninterrupted back and forth between people and the land. In this cycle of prosperity, a relationship to land directly benefits people and culture; and the resulting attitudes and perceptions, in turn, positively affect land and nature. It is a cycle of sympathy, mutuality, service, and reward.

We might better call this new expression of land conservation "relationship conservation." Relationship should be what drives and guides land conservation: interdependencies between people, between species, between the whole of the land community. Through this new lens, our actions with the land will be right or wrong not because a law tells us so but because they either enhance or diminish our opportunity for relationships with all that lives on the land. A positive act of land conservation is one that strengthens the relationship between people and the land and the values taught by that relationship. A negative, or at best neutral, act of land conservation is one that does not.

The quality and character of the connections that we can have to place and to one another are as diverse as the land itself. For example, our relationship with wilderness shows our forbearance and respect; our relationship to a working ranch speaks of our commitment, and patience. From the stories I've been told, it is evident how our strengths as a people emerge from the quality of our relationships with the land, including our sense of care, well being, neighborliness, trustworthiness, and health. It is equally clear how many of our weaknesses as a culture grow from our inability to develop a connection with place.

SAVING LAND, SAVING RELATIONSHIPS

Lynn Sherrod sits across from us with her back to a large picture window that allows us to look straight out across hundreds of acres of pasture to distant Elk Mountain near Routt National Forest in northwestern Colorado. A band of large cottonwoods lining

Ranch disintegration
Yampa Valley
Colorado

the Elk River cuts through the middle of this view. Lynn was born and raised in this valley and her grandmother homesteaded on the flats nearby. Now Lynn runs a commercial cow-calf operation with her husband, Delbert. They have worked this specific piece of land for nearly twenty-five years, and Lynn can't stop herself from turning and gazing out over the ranch every few minutes. It is constantly in her mind, in her vision of the world.

One of Lynn's hobbies, in part to keep her sanity, is to take pictures of FOR SALE signs and the huge ranch gates that have sprung up in Elk Valley over the last ten years. Steamboat Springs, twenty minutes up the road, was once a cow town filled with homesteaders and ranchers but is now home to millionaires and weekend skiers. A 240-acre ranch abutting the Sherrods' land sold, sight unseen, over the Internet for $10,000 an acre. (It wasn't a rancher who bought that land.) A 3,500-acre spread that had been a cornerstone of the ranching community sold for $10.2 million to an investor from California. The good news, Lynn told us, is that the new owner has put a conservation easement over the ranch. There's part of Lynn that is particularly happy about this, because she and her fellow ranchers in Elk Valley are the force behind the Colorado Cattlemen's Land Trust, one of the country's first land protection organizations to emerge from the traditional ranching community. She believes that the fragmentation of working ranches into recreational "ranchettes" is killing her community. Keeping the land in large parcels protects the opportunity for ranching in the future. It's also very positive for biodiversity. But she has another concern. She knows that a conservation easement may protect the land but won't necessarily protect the culture that has lived on and loved that land.

One rancher told us, "Second-home people don't come here to be neighbors, they come here to get away." By this, she didn't intend to be unfriendly but merely to point out the reality that the investor from California won't be likely to volunteer on the local school board or ambulance squad, be available to help Lynn and

Fetcher Ranch
Yampa Valley
Colorado

Delbert get their hay in, be willing to swap machinery, or even get their mail at the local post office. Lynn is acutely aware that their land trust, in the process of saving land, may be creating a museum for a way life that once was—and that it's her own life that will be on display. These are Lynn's words:

> This is an incredibly beautiful place and one of the reasons it's still really beautiful is because there's been a group of people who have spent their lifeblood working to keep it this way. We love what we do, and this land has us by the throat. I don't want to try to make it sound like too spiritual of a relationship, but it really is. You have to respect it more than anything else. If it's just a commodity or if it's just a dollar sign or if it's just a crop, it won't ever mean the same thing to you and it won't ever be as productive for you. Because you've got to care about it more than anything else in your life, which is what these guys do. Like I said, it has us by the throat; this love that we have for this piece of ground is hard to understand. You can't legislate morality. You can't legislate love. You can't legislate a sense of caring. If it's not there, it's not there. It's one thing to protect the land for perpetuity and keep it whole, but if you can't protect our ability to stay on the land, what's the point? We can have all the land protected in the world, and I don't know what good it's going to do us. When the people who really know and understand and love that land and manage it are taken off of it, so you've saved it, but what have you saved it for?

The community of Yampa Valley is a powerful place to consider the success of conservation in terms of relationships. Much of the Yampa Valley is surrounded by public land managed either by the Forest Service or by the Bureau of Land Management. I asked several people to explain the difference between ranchland and public land. To a person, the differences were described not in terms of the quality of the land but the quality of the relationship. Jay Fetcher, a rancher along the Elk River, told us, "We feel a life-long responsibility to our land, while you're never more than a visitor to public land. This land is us, so we take much better care of it." Another rancher in an adjoining valley said, "one relationship is about appreciation and the other is about responsibility. I think most folks really appreciate the national forest, but this land here is in my blood. I am responsible for it."

Buried not too far below the fear of loss expressed so poignantly by many ranchers in the Yampa Valley is a fundamental hope that relationships with the land will improve, and that their own lives will not be replaced with lifestyles. They hope the second-home owners moving in from away will join the community and search out something for themselves beyond the romantic notions of cowboys and gorgeous vistas. Those people who knew the valley the way it once was are hoping that the newcomers' relationship with the land matures into something bigger than their own dreams for a certain lifestyle. Susan Otis, who runs a local land trust in the valley, put it this way: "It's a little confusing right now. Some of the new landowners may actually have better land practices and their resources may enable them to do more good than we expect. Some of the conservation buyers are not that distant from agriculture. Who am I to say that the next generation isn't going to be even more responsible than who is on the land today?" What isn't confusing is the reality that saving the land, alone, isn't going to get the ranchers the future they yearn for, but saving relationships and building new ones might. In the Yampa Valley and everywhere else, the value of that relationship to the land might best be measured by the extent to which it evolves beyond self-interest. All healthy relationships entail sacrifice and are never solely about what makes one person feel good, but are about what's also good for someone else. Relationship implies a responsibility that goes beyond one's own dreams. Wendell Berry put it this way: "to grow up is to go beyond our inborn selfishness and arrogance; to be grown up is to know that the self is not a place to live."

THE FEAR OF KNOWING ONE ANOTHER

I have a friend who has created a unique way of life on a stretch of coastline in Down East Maine. For over forty years, Bill Coperthwaite has encouraged the growth of spruce by pulling fir saplings by hand, transplanted *Rosa rugosa,* built osprey nests, harvested mussels, and built a handsome home of wood without a road or electricity or plumbing. The land comprising Bill's homestead has been gently shaped by his great strength, vision, and love. It is simple, respectful, well designed, and practical. Bill rarely travels all of this coastline but he deeply appreciates it as completely wild. Much of this landscape he owns, and the rests he just hopes the best for. Bill's relationship to Dickinson's Reach has been a great education for me. Over the years, I have come to understand how Bill and the land have prospered together in undeniable ways; his relationship to that place represents to me a high human achievement.

Beginning four years ago, Bill's home began to change dramatically. One summer he heard earth-moving equipment pushing over trees across the bay. A developer from Connecticut was constructing a four-mile-long road that would open up a wild peninsula adjacent to Bill's land. By the end of the year, a subdivision was filed that would create fourteen new summer homes. A year later, Bill started seeing helicopters flying overhead on a regular basis, and he noticed motorboats moored off the coast just south of his property line. Bill soon learned that a developer from Detroit had filed plans to build a luxury golf course and vacation homes on the land that is his source of drinking water.

Even as we are working to protect both of these properties and

Dickinson's Reach
Machias Bay
Maine

stop the development, we know the same problem will quickly present itself elsewhere. It's hypocritical for conservationists to oppose all forms of development when our own lives depend on changing the land somewhere. And since conservation can't keep pace with development, what counts is how and where we protect the land and how we raise the awareness of those who seek to change it. The quality of how we use the land will improve significantly when all developers become as aware and responsive to as many relationships with the land as they can. Conservationists, therefore, have the same obligations as developers: to respect and improve the quality of *all* relationships with the land. I want to see our culture heal, to go to the root of the problem, and that means encouraging every relationship with the land to evolve.

Does looking at Bill's challenge through the lens of relationships give me any hope of solving the problem? And, to ask a more painful question, will Bill's way of life survive if the golf course development succeeds? I want to claim that Bill's relationship with the land is more "right," less destructive, and more valuable than that of others who seek to change this coastline, forever altering the life there, in order to play a game. I want desperately for my sense of what's right to prevail and, yet, I also want a dialogue. How might Bill's stewardship compare with this man's stewardship? How do we tell right and wrong and all the shades of gray in between? What might Bill and the Detroit developer have to teach one another? The moral and ethical judgments necessary in order to have a conservation movement guided by relationship are exceedingly hard to make, which is exactly why we have not yet made them—and exactly why the conflict keeps coming up over and over again. It is impossible to have a shared ethic without engaging in the debate. I want a world in which Bill's life has something to teach the developer from Detroit.

Lynn Sherrod knows that an honorable relationship between humans is the same as an honorable relationship between people and the land—that is, one in which it is right to use the word *love.* Building such a relationship is a delicate process of refining the truths that we can tell each other. It requires risking being vulnerable and breaking down our walls of self-delusion and isolation. It is important to have such relationships to place and to other people as a way of doing justice to our complexity. These are Lynn's words:

> My husband's an incredible person, and the land benefits. And if you can pass that love and that passion on to the next generation, then we've done our job. And if we don't . . . if we don't imbue somebody else with that spirit of why it's important to keep the land whole, then we're all lost. Because that land doesn't have a chance of going on. If we lose that respect and that sacredness of that point of view about keeping the land whole at any cost, then we become challenged in our ability to conduct ourselves as people into the future. I believe that with every breath I take. And I suppose it's like loving another person. Somebody that you have the right and the willingness to love and they love you back, then you're going to invest yourself wholly in that relationship. You're going to be much more careful in that relationship if you feel like it won't ever be returned. And the land loves you back, it does. If you're allowed to care for it and do what's right, it loves you back by being productive and healthy and taking care of you. Everything you do, every breath you breathe has to be about maintaining the viability of that land so it can keep going on, giving back for generations to come.

Viewing land conservation as the conservation of relationships forces our culture to become more aware of itself, because the only way to make choices between right and wrong is to debate together—much more than we have—to determine what our culture needs in order to be healthy and to act out of wisdom.

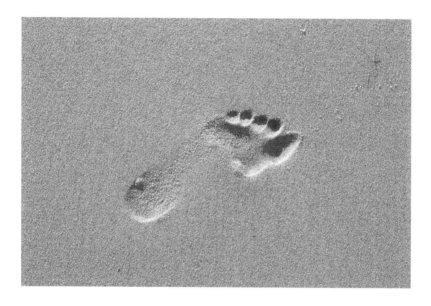

Olympic National Park
Makah Lands
Washington

What sort of natural habitats—from wilderness to riparian corridors to working landscapes—do we humans need in order to create a healthy, responsible culture? What are the forces in our world that make our culture unhealthy?

These changes to Bill's home have been deeply painful and threatening to me, yet they have also tested my compassion for those with whom I disagree the most. I must trust that every person holds the potential for a shared sense of an evolving and maturing relationship with the land. I ask myself how I might approach the golf course developer with an appreciation that he longs for something on that land. Is there a good that can come from his longing? I read in the newspaper how he chose this particular stretch of remote Maine coastline because of its beauty, because he loved it. Love seems a more promising starting place for discussion than does economics or science.

We are all stewards of the land, so we might re-imagine our work as creating all the possible doorways through which we and our neighbors might walk to begin to mature our relationship to the land. The doorways through which we might access this path and begin an evolving relationship with the whole land community include:

RECREATION: hiking, climbing, canoeing, bird-watching, sport hunting and fishing

WORK: land restoration and remediation, farming, hunting and fishing, forestry, urban gardening

AESTHETICS: observing and appreciating beauty, complexity, and the wholeness of life

HUMAN SPIRIT: gaining inspiration from land and a closer connection to one's source of values

INTELLECTUAL KNOWLEDGE: reading, writing and borrowing wisdom from biology, ecology, anthropology, sociology, economics, ecopsychology, city planning

Of course, there are good relationships and bad relationships and infinite shades in between, but there is a line that divides the two, which is defined by self-interest, or exploitation. One begins a relationship when one begins to think beyond one's own needs and wants.

Once on the path, there are thousands of different possible relationships—changing and maturing—leading to the great prosperity of both people and the land. All these relationships fall somewhere between stewardship, the ethic that aspires to live close to the land in a mutually nurturing way, and forbearance, the ethic that allows us to sacrifice our needs so that other life can flourish. A model for relationships with the land might look something like this:

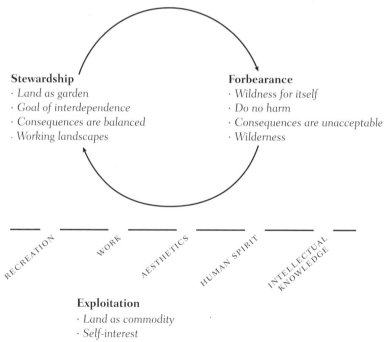

Stewardship
· *Land as garden*
· *Goal of interdependence*
· *Consequences are balanced*
· *Working landscapes*

Forbearance
· *Wildness for itself*
· *Do no harm*
· *Consequences are unacceptable*
· *Wilderness*

RECREATION   WORK   AESTHETICS   HUMAN SPIRIT   INTELLECTUAL KNOWLEDGE

Exploitation
· *Land as commodity*
· *Self-interest*
· *Consequences are largely denied*
· *Industrial forestry and agribusiness, sprawl*

Every human being is complex and unique, and requires his or her own journey. For some, that path may start as a love of rock climbing, or gardening, and for others it may begin with a way of life that brings them closest to their highest values. All doorways are acceptable, as long as we commit to a path of evolving and deepening our relationship with the land. It seems evident, too, that there are conditions that amplify these experiences for all of us; for example, any of these experiences of connection when made as a young child or in some fashion of close community are bound to be the most powerful and enduring.

Doug Wade wrote back to Aldo Leopold and said, "We need some new philosophies to guide us. So far, Aldo, you are one of the few wildlife men who has attempted to give us some new guideposts and objectives, some thoughts that have disturbed our complacency." One new guidepost that Leopold offered was to urge his fellow conservationists to see the whole, not just their own small part of the world. Leopold was asking us to be aware, to be truly mindful of what was happening around us. The hunters wanted more deer, the fishermen wanted more salmon, and the loggers wanted more trees, even if each had to destroy one for the benefit of the other.

That's old thinking, or is it? Even today doesn't the wilderness advocate want more wilderness and the stewardship advocate want more working landscapes? How often do you hear one advocating and working for the other? Most of us have not yet found the vision to see that a healthy life requires a relationship to other healthy life. We long for a bold vision that makes seamless and whole the story of how Classie Parker working the soil in Harlem is connected to Bill Coperthwaite paddling the wild coast of Dickinson's Reach in Maine. We hunger to understand the complexity of all the ways of living in between because it offers us the chance to make our own lives whole. To live fully, people need a direct relationship to nature in working landscapes, in state parks, in urban gardens and in millions of backyards. And, yet, we must also culti-

Little Kennebec Bay
Machias Bay
Maine

vate the wild in our own nature by ensuring the complete wildness in some parts of the land. Today, it's not clear that anyplace is beyond the reach of our dominant ideology, which makes our acts of awareness and restraint even more important, even more profound. Without wilderness, there will be no place for the nonhuman world to live fully. And for us, achieving a relationship to both working landscapes and wilderness is the only way to find that state of communion with the world for which we all hunger.

A great lesson was taught to me recently by a senior colleague at TPL who said during a retreat, "How do I live with what I cannot do?" We can only try to accept gracefully our own inadequacies while doing the best that we can, and embrace the fact that everything changes. Nothing is permanent; nothing, truly, can be set aside in perpetuity. This is difficult for many conservationists to accept; their idealism leads them to want to save the world by keeping things as they are today. But when all species die, they bequeath to their successors a slightly changed environment. All of our religions and philosophies and all of our scientific understandings acknowledge change. The land will change, by our own hands or not, and some of the places we love will be lost, but if our relationships to the earth are ever gaining in insight and leading us to new awareness, we can restore portions of what has been lost. We can make amends. If we can accept the idea of impermanence—that all life does change—we might be better prepared to focus on our relationship to land as much as we focus on the land itself. In this new light, land conservation would have as part of its mission the notions of sympathy, building health and well being, and reducing suffering much more than the goal of keeping land the same.

If a butterfly's disturbance of the air in East Africa can lead to a storm system six weeks later in New England, why can't the same sort of transformation happen in our culture? Scientists call the butterfly effect "sensitive dependence on critical conditions," and I believe it can happen in our human lives. It happened to me. The

Five Star Garden
Manhattan Island
New York

briefest introductions to new ways of living and to this new radical center for land conservation changed how I aspire to live. Suke and Bill Coperthwaite and Classie Parker, among many others, have made their own lives infinitely richer by achieving a proximity to their own source of inspiration. And each of them brought this meaning and purpose into their lives through a brave and unexpected commitment to a relationship with the land. Just being with them, sometimes for as short as a day, has helped me to live differently and to evolve my view of the purpose of land conservation.

Rainer Maria Rilke, the German poet and philosopher, wrote, "there is somewhere an ancient enmity between our daily lives and the Great Work." Mahatma Gandhi called this the "dissonance between deed and creed," and it was reading Thoreau while in jail in 1908 that inspired his words. Thoreau's own response to the need for healing any rift between action and belief was to seek nature on the banks of Walden Pond. So this is, indeed, a very old and recurring story for humans. We know deep in our hearts what is the Great Work. It is a moral cry to declare that we want to live differently, that we want to express our love and our prosperity in terms of the quality of our relationships, not in the amount we acquire and consume.

WHAT DOES SUCCESS LOOK LIKE?

I have heard others say that we are on the brink of a Great Forgetting, a point where our relationships are so fractured that we have almost forgotten why they were important in the first place. We have nearly said the final good-bye, having long since shaken hands, and are just now waiting to shut the door. But not quite. We hear a piece of music and feel a deep unexplained stirring inside of us. We climb a mountain in the fall and are swept away by the beauty. Our love for this land, this life—all life—has us by the throat even when we don't have the words to speak.

Atalaya Mountain
Sangre de Cristo foothills
New Mexico

I prefer to believe that we are on the brink of a Great Remembering, a time when America's prosperity allows us to reconsider what matters most to us, when we are punished enough by sprawl and the loss of life that we can find the bravery to show self-restraint and self-love. The path to the great remembering is through the healing of land conservation and the healing of ourselves, through a million different ways to show our forbearance and to reconnect with the life that is around us.

This aspiration for land conservation as creating relationships is not another strategy by environmentalists to find new constituencies to meet political or fundraising objectives. It's a way to lead with our morals first, to radically re-invent the objectives of why guarding and loving something like land is important for humans to do. It is the path for land conservation to speak more directly to peoples' lives:

- What does land conservation say to young families who are worried about the quality of the food they bring to their table?
- What do we say to parents who wonder where and how their children will play?
- What do we say to the father who wants his daughter to see and hear songbirds in the spring?
- What do we say to all women whose breast milk is toxic?
- What do we say to the communities that have grown up alongside rivers that they've never been able to walk beside, never been able to get to know outside of fear?
- What do we say to the husband and wife who have dedicated the best of themselves to farming a piece of land and who can no longer afford to remain there?
- How do we explain to our children that a species that has lived on this earth during our lifetime may not survive their lifetime?

We say there is much that can be done in this moment in your life. We say that we have practical strategies for the daily work of land conservation that shows our sympathy and compassion, as well as our proven ability to rebuild straw by straw, moment by moment, our frail connections with the land. We have strategies that enable every town in America to have an organic community-supported farm. We want to assure every person that there is a park and safe place to experience the natural world within an easy walk of his or her home, no matter if that person lives in Des Moines or Oakland. We can make it possible—even in south central Los Angeles or on Euclid Avenue in Chicago—for everyone to grow some portion of his or her own food. We will try to ensure, in the Yampa Valley of Colorado, that there will always be a culture of people living off the land, where that relationship is best defined by work and affection; and in the Mendocino Headlands of California, we will help create small economies that understand the land's frailty and abundance. We will help make clear that the LA River can be no less loved than the Rogue River in Oregon even though one is channeled in cement and the other is called "wild and scenic." We say you were meant to be here.

As an example of just one region of the country, I am enthralled by a vision for my native New England that is possible through this view of conservation as building relationships. New England has 450 land conservation organizations that could easily fulfill this vision in half the time and with 10 percent of the money it has taken to build a new underground highway across one mile of Boston.

Here are some themes that might guide that work:

FOOD What we eat and drink is our most important daily relationship to the land. Given that one-quarter of America's land base is in some form of agriculture and that the far majority of this is industrial and destructive of both land and people, the single most important change that land conservationists can make is

Sante Fe Farmer's Market
Sangre de Cristo foothills
New Mexico

to focus on improving how we grow healthy, local food. We can use our skills and resources to better support farmers who use nature as the measure. Land conservation can help good farming by helping to keep farms affordable and intact, by encouraging community-supported agriculture and organic farms. We can support good harvesting practices on land and water by using our money and skills to keep access affordable, to financially support cooperatives of green producers, and to use our land to keep community intact. Something is terribly broken when Maine, once New England's breadbasket, must now import 70 percent of its food. We can celebrate food that is unique to our regions, food that says something about us and reminds us that ours is like no other place in the world.

MOVEMENT We are a migratory species, and the fullness of our souls is reached when we can see and feel our landscape on our own scale. The ability to walk, bike, ride horseback, and canoe the furthest possible distances creates a sense of freedom that is not unlike wildness, even though these activities might take us through a suburb or even a city. And the same need for movement and migration applies to the more-than-human world that needs wildlife corridors. Experiencing the land using our own muscles, moving at a slower pace than we normally do, and engaging our sight and smell and consciousness make us loyal to that place. Largely as result of Benton MacKaye's 1921 vision for a continuous Appalachian Trail from Georgia to Maine, there are now many other footpaths, greenways, ski trails, and kayaking and canoe trails that allow Americans to cover hundreds of miles of their native region by their own ingenuity and knowledge of the land. New Englanders are close to an integrated vision that allows someone who lives in Boston to be able to walk on a trail from Boston Harbor to the summit of Mount Katahdin in Maine.

HISTORY History defines the difference between land and place—place being the union of land with people and their stories. By conserving places out of our past, we learn metaphors and stories that help us find our way in the future. Because of this relationship granted to us through an act of conservation, we have the opportunity for pathos, memory, and connection. We show humility and respect by conserving a historic cabin, an earlier expression of how to live, or a creation from the past, not because we hope to stop change but because these are the milestones of our progress, examples of what we have loved and struggled over. In protecting a 200-year-old boat shop, or one of the last herring smokehouses, or the boyhood home of Dr. Martin Luther King, we interject into the conservation of natural resources the story of social resources. Critical questions emerge that shape and guide us. What is the role of work and way of life to conservationists? What is the connection between civil rights and the environment?

DIVERSITY We need biological diversity on the planet for the same reasons we need all forms of diversity. Diversity creates empathy, stability, and morality. Simply put, we cannot know unity without first knowing diversity. Land conservation strikes an essential chord of meaning and fairness when it explicitly promotes diversity of all types: biological, cultural, racial, and socioeconomic. To live by a credo of diversity, conservationists must work in diverse geographies, serve diverse peoples, be sympathetic to diverse relationships with the land, seek to work beyond the boundaries of their mission, and be constituted of diverse peoples. Through our work, we are always transferring to the public not just land but empowerment itself. At the heart of land conservation, by definition, is the obligation that all involved look beyond their immediate families to the needs of the larger community. Conservation, therefore, is first and foremost, against self-interest. And if land conservation is about citizenship, then it must equally be about changing existing power structures. Even when we protect a small pond in a remote part of a town, we should be thinking about how this can create profound change in that community. Through this fundamental commitment to diversity, conservation builds awareness, strength, and principle.

GOOD WORK Whether carried out by a logger in a forest or a lawyer in an office tower, all forms of work ultimately affect the land. In this important sense, no one is divorced from the land and all share equally in its future. The conservation movement is quick to talk about recreation but is most often silent on work. Yet, the place where we live and the work that we do forge many of our beliefs. Good work is fundamental to the human experience and, therefore, a critical component of any conservation philosophy that hopes to influence our culture. For land conservationists to promote good work, we need to use our resources to aid what remains of our land-based culture. Simultaneously, we need to allow examples of good work to thrive on our "protected" landscapes. We need to constantly search for projects that go beyond recreation or leisure to encompass how people provide for themselves. Some conservation organizations are espousing notions of good work by protecting farmland or allowing green timber harvesting on their lands. Others are investing in fishing and farming cooperatives and making small financial loans to build businesses along greenways. These activities build deeper human relationships with the whole land community by demonstrating how all types of work can reinforce people's connection to the land.

One of the most important steps that the conservation community can take is to redefine notions of success. Our society's fixation with numbers isn't unusual, but it should be readily apparent by now that one tends to become what one measures. The perfect example of this is the degree to which our gross national product —a calculation based entirely on economic growth—tends to significantly diminish our own estimation of other attributes that might make us successful as a people, attributes like the quality

Local catch, Halawa Valley
Molokai
Hawaii

of our air and water, the education of our citizens, the state of our healthcare system. We measure economic growth; therefore economic growth is our primary purpose. Likewise, the purpose and value of land conservation is significantly diminished when it is measured only in terms of acres saved and dollars raised.

The cultural historian Thomas Berry wrote, "It's all a question of story. We are in trouble now because we don't have a good story. We are in between stories. The old story is no longer effective." So let us now begin the exciting work of creating and telling that new story. The protagonist is the yearning for a better life—a new American dream—that lies within the human heart and soul. Conservation is the pathway along which our protagonist hopes for a good and noble conclusion. And the storytellers are all the people who have risked entering into a shared sense of love, a shared sense of an evolving and maturing relationship with all of the inhabitants of the land. Lynn Sherrod tells us her story about living among the sandhill cranes of the Yampa Valley:

> Sandhill cranes are very, very shy and they're very hard to get close to. And they're really big birds. One morning, I just wanted to hang out with my husband so I went out on chores with him. He was over in the field working on a solar charger for the fence line. Then I heard two cranes—they mate for life—and they were calling back and forth to each other and they have this real kind of haunting rattling cry and I love it in the morning in the summertime. We always have our windows open and it's the first thing I hear every morning and to me that will be one of the most special sounds of my entire life. Especially as it echoes across the valley. It's beautiful. And I could hear these two cranes calling to each other because Del was near their space. And he couldn't see them but I watched him walk right through the middle of them, and they were probably only fifteen feet apart. Neither one of them ever flew; they

kept calling back and forth. Del was so low-key, doing his work slowly, he was so much a part of what they were used to that they all co-existed. To me, that's what it's all about.

Our concern for the Earth should be the same as our concern for own heart and soul. This is why land conservation must search to see the results of its labor in both nature and culture. Our struggle as conservationists is that we have consistently responded to the Earth's cry for help with technical or political solutions such as "saving" land and passing new laws. While it is clear that we must do these things, it is also clear how inadequate they are as lasting solutions. What then is the moral response that land conservation must make? I believe it is to rethink the promise of land conservation as the defense of all things worth loving in this world. This aspiration for land conservation will be not reached alone by how much nature we can put aside, but by how much love and respect for the land we can engender in the greatest number of people. Our greatest achievement is not being able to say "we saved this place," but being able to say, instead, "you belong here." Land conservation can become the story of how the soul of the land became the soul of our culture, signaling over and over our place in the world.

A PLACE TO BEGIN

As I write about these aspirations, I feel like a child walking upstream from stone to stone, unsure of the exact path and slipping more than once. Each step is based on part experience, part intuition, and part blind faith. I have so few answers, and yet I am compelled to offer questions, and a way to begin. I am moved by what I do not know. I thereby wish to conclude by inviting you into the dialogue, and by offering some basic principles for how we might define conservation success in terms of building relationships. I can envision each of these criteria being greatly improved and expanded upon by hundreds of conservationists, until one day, years from now, we have a new framework for guiding and measuring the success of land conservation in building relationships between land and people.

We have been successful if *the process of conserving land* . . .

· Creates new alliances that would not otherwise exist

. Expands individual choice in a community

· Brings opposing forces together

· Helps a community to be more self-aware

· Enables a community to address other fundamental issues of life such as education, justice, and common welfare

· Expands the public sphere by raising the standard of citizenship

· Creates generational connections within a community

· Transforms the existing power structure

· Removes the insulation between people, and between people and nature

· Teaches an alternative story to prevailing mainstream culture by providing the example of forbearance and self-restraint

· Contributes directly to the health and well being of the whole land community

· Helps people to inhabit their place differently, to dwell and imagine their lives differently

We have been successful if *the conserved land itself* . . .

· Provides the community with a viable sense of dependence on all that is local

- Provides examples of human relationships to the land that are more than economic
- Provides for basic food needs and teaches about growing food
- Affords people a place to be themselves, to have fun, to be joyful

- Becomes the place where people feel safe and motivated to work out their conflicts
- Protects the natural features and the most enduring ways of life that are unique to that area: the distinct flora and fauna, the watersheds and mountain ranges

- Defines the region by nature, not legislature
- Creates a safe setting for interaction with other species, countering the extinction of human experience
- Provides a historical perspective on the life and struggle of those who came before

- Enables meaningful work to exist in an honorable relationship to nature
- Protects biological diversity thus strengthening the total diversity and whole community health
- Provides a space for people to explore their own physical strengths and weaknesses
- Provides a space for families to be together without human or technological distraction

- Enhances the aesthetic appeal of the community, thus improving the local quality of all life
- Creates more opportunity for people to have direct experiences of the natural world and the wild
- Creates opportunities for cross-enchantment between people who have different, direct experiences of nature

THE PRACTICE OF LISTENING

———

The cold waters of Tebenkof Bay lap against my legs as I stare down into a tidal pool. At first, I see nothing other than rock and kelp, but patience slowly reveals forms and colors. Then I am startled by the presence of movement everywhere. The barnacles are feeding in the current. Almost every small shell starts to move and becomes a creature. The beautiful pattern of reds, browns, grays, and whites becomes twenty-five different crabs. The long piece of kelp, I now see, is food for hundreds of tiny fish. I am no longer blind.

Two ravens fly up the beach toward me, and as they pass overhead I can hear the beating of their wings and the exhalation of their breath. Later that afternoon, friends and I sit by a fire on the beach listening to sea otters crack shells on their stomachs. At dusk, a flock of geese flies overhead, calling out to us. As I lie down to sleep on the gravel beach, I hear the soft but constant beating of a drum coming to me from the islands across the bay. It echoes in my ears with the sound of the winter wren and the loon and the no-see-ums, and I realize it is the beating of my own heart.

What I found so moving in Tebenkof Bay was not its wildness, but its completeness. More than any other place I've been, this place feels full of life. The humpback whales are there and the black bear and the eagles and the wolves and the massive schools of salmon are there. In every inlet, they are there. But also there is the ancient totem pole left by the Clingkit people that we found still standing, held by the branches of a hundred-year-old Sitka spruce. And I'm thankful that we are there, and for how we are there: traveling in kayaks, respecting the silence, leaving no trace.

Being in Tebenkof Bay for just a week made us different people than when we arrived. We need to protect this awareness, this sympathy we have for one another and all of the life here, as much as we need to protect the place itself. Seeing Tebenkof Bay through the eyes of *listening and being aware* made me want to return to my own home and love it better, to be a better father, and a better member of my own community.

Traveling to southeast Alaska helped me see the connection between the experience of the wild and what we are now engaged in learning at TPL. We are engaged in contemplating and exploring our greater purpose as an organization. It is the journey of becoming more self-aware. It is the practice of listening. And we know that we cannot find self-awareness within TPL without first seeing it in ourselves. Three years ago, TPL began an exercise in discovering our highest values by having open discussions about our mission, by exploring our individual lives and motivations, by bringing into our community the best thinkers and social critics, and by adopting several important tools that have helped us think and see more clearly. For example, over forty of our staff have participated in weeklong retreats in the wilderness that combine silence, meditation, and discussion. It is through this practice, and the discipline of our everyday work, that we have begun to envision a new future.

Albert Einstein said, "You cannot solve a problem with the same consciousness that created it." We have encouraged an environment of learning that will enable us to overcome the inevitable obstacles that might keep us from acting on our values. This journey continues to ask each of us what in our own life requires healing, why our culture struggles, and how our work in land conservation has the potential to heal our country and ourselves. The practice of *listening and being aware* is helping us to develop the humility, sense of fairness, and wider view of the world necessary to create the magnitude of change that we aspire to. This is a time for reflection *and* absolute boldness. This is a time to experiment without sacrificing any discipline. This is a time when we must allow what we care about most to guide everything we do. To be wild, they say, is to be bold, untamed, and free. This is a time for us to practice our wildness.

FOR FURTHER READING

Berry, Wendell. 2000. *Life is a Miracle*. Washington, D.C: Counterpoint Press.

————. 1981. *Recollected Essays 1965–1980*. San Francisco: North Point Press.

————. 1998. *The Selected Poems of Wendell Berry*. Washington, D.C: Counterpoint Press.

————. 1992. *Sex, Economy, Freedom and Community*. New York: Pantheon.

————. 1995. *Another Turn of the Crank*. Washington, D.C: Counterpoint Press.

————. 1989. *The Hidden Wound*. San Francisco: North Point Press.

Bookchin, Murray. 1982. *The Ecology of Freedom*. Palo Alto: Cheshire Books.

Cronon, William. 1983. *Changes in the Land: Indians, Colonists, and the Ecology of New England*. New York: Hill and Wang.

Dillard, Annie. 1982. *Teaching a Stone to Talk*. New York: Harper and Row.

Eisenberg, Evan. 1998. *The Ecology of Eden*. New York: Alfred A. Knopf.

Fischer, Louis. 1950. *The Life of Mahatma Gandhi*. New York: Harper and Row.

Freyfogle, Eric. 2001. *New Agrarianism*. Washington, D.C.: Island Press.

————. 2000. "A Sand County Almanac at 50." *ELR News and Analysis*. Washington, D.C.

————. 1998. *Bounded People, Boundless Lands*. Washington, D.C.: Shearwater Press/Island Press.

Hogan, Linda. 1995. *Dwellings*. New York: W. W. Norton.

Kellert, Stephen R. 1997. *Kinship to Mastery: Biophilia in Human Evolution and Development*. Washington, D.C.: Island Press

Kemmis, Daniel. 1995. *The Good City and the Good Life*. New York: Houghton Mifflin.

Kunstler, James Howard. 1993. *The Geography of Nowhere: The Rise and Decline of America's Man-Made Landscape*. New York: Simon and Schuster.

Leopold, Aldo. 1986. *A Sand County Almanac*. New York: Ballentine Books (New York: Oxford University Press, 1966).

Logsdon, Gene. 1993. *The Contrary Farmer*. Post Mills, Vermont: Chelsea Green Publishing.

Macy, Joanna. 1991. *World as Lover, World as Self*. Berkeley, California: Parallax Press.

McKibben, Bill. "How Much is Enough? The Environmental Movement as a Pivot in Human History." Harvard Seminar on Environmental Values, October 2000.

Meadows, Donella H. 1991. *The Global Citizen*. Washington, D.C.: Island Press.

Nabhan, Gary Paul. 1997. *Cultures of Habitat*. Washington, D.C.: Counterpoint Press.

Nash, Roderick. 1989. *The Rights of Nature*. Madison: University of Wisconsin Press.

Nearing, Helen, and Scott Nearing. 1954. *Living the Good Life: How to Live Sanely and Simply in a Troubled World*. New York: Shocken Books.

Pollan, Michael. 1991. *Second Nature*. New York: Atlantic Monthly Press.

Pyle, Robert Michael. 1993. *The Thunder Tree*. New York: The Lyons Press.

Sanders, Scott Russell. 1993. "Staying Put." *Orion Magazine*, Vol. 4.

Schumacher, E. F. 1979. *Good Work.* New York: Harper and Row.

Snyder, Gary. 1990. *The Practice of the Wild.* San Francisco: North Point Press.

————. 1995. *A Place in Space.* Washington, D.C.: Counterpoint Press.

Stegner, Wallace. 1998. *Marking the Sparrow's Fall: Wallace Stegner's American West.* New York: Henry Holt.

Swimme, Brian. 1996. *The Hidden Heart of the Cosmos.* Maryknoll, New York: Orbis Books.

Thoreau, Henry David. 1958. *Walden.* New York: Harper Classics (Boston: Houghton Mifflin, 1854).

Turner, Jack. 1996. *The Abstract Wild.* Tucson: University of Arizona Press.

White, Richard. 1995. "Are You an Environmentalist, or Do You Work for a Living?" In *Uncommon Ground,* edited by William Cronon. New York: W. W. Norton: 239–243.

ACKNOWLEDGMENTS

Researching and writing this essay has been a long exploration, and I am grateful to the many individuals who have made the journey less lonely and made these ideas far more complete. Many of the stories I share with readers would not have come to me, nor would they have happy endings, without the extraordinary work of my colleagues at the Trust for Public Land: Badge Blackett, Bowen Blair, Margaret Eadington, Deb Love, Ted Harrison, Kelly Huddleston, Susan Ives, Teresa McHugh, Jennifer Melville, Doug Nash, Scott Parker, Al Raymond, Geoff Roach, Andy Stone, Steve Thompson, Kate Williams, Tim Wirth, and Jeremy Wintersteen. These people and their many TPL colleagues across the country work tirelessly every day with communities to protect what is most loved. While their work is community-based it is also hope-based, and my intent is to honor their good work by suggesting herein a larger meaning and significance of that great endeavor.

Much of my own awareness of this larger meaning of our work grew directly out of being welcomed into many people's homes, listening, and sharing stories. A deep bow of gratitude to all those who shared their lives and their thinking with me: Horace Axtell, Craig Barnes, Kate Botham, Suby Bowden, Greg Brown, Grove Barnett, Miguel Chavez, Bill Coperthwaite, Kathy and Glenn Davis, Jean Driscoll, Jay Fetcher, Bill Gay, Carla HighEagle, Kurt Hoelt, Levi Holt, Keith Lawrence, Classie Parker, Bill Pickard, Jaime Pinkham, Lynn Sherrod, John Reppun, Dean Rossi, Richard Skorman, Linda Velarde, Jamie Williams, and Pat Wortman.

Ann Armbrecht, both a great writer and a wise cultural anthropologist, traveled with me to many of these communities, and this essay reflects her own enormous understanding of the land and community life as well as her training as a sensitive observer of people. Our long discussions of the recurring issues that we witnessed together became some of the themes of this essay and I am indebted to Ann for her own contribution to new ways of thinking about land conservation. I also owe an enormous intellectual debt to Julianne Newton who knocked on my door one summer day and quickly became a trusted and important ally in the writing of this essay and then, furthermore, in the creation of the Center for Land and People. As both my research assistant and my teacher, Julianne's training and her own keen observations have enriched my work immeasurably. Kathi Anderson and Helen Bowdoin of the Walden Woods Project forced me to organize my thinking in a very helpful manner by inviting me to give three talks at their remarkable Thoreau Institute in Concord, Massachusetts. My thanks also to Jenna Dixon and Ann Aspell for helping to design and produce this book.

The Educational Foundation of America and the Nathan Cummings Foundation provided the funding not only for producing this book and the research that was required to bring it together, but also for a host of other outreach efforts all designed to help rethink the promise of land conservation. Without their leadership and risk-taking, this work simply would not exist. I can offer no greater acknowledgment of my thanks.

Will Rogers, the president of the Trust for Public Land, cleared the path for serious and fruitful discussions about the larger purpose of land conservation that started at TPL and is now spreading across the entire conservation movement. Will has led this risky process of evolution with quiet strength, keen determination, and the contribution of his own personal beliefs and credibility.

I also want to thank Richard Nelson for the example of his writing and his love of life and for the encouragement he has given me to speak through stories. I owe great thanks to Terry Tempest Williams, who urged me to dig deeper, to avoid the old polarities, and to find the radical center. John Elder's great intellect and graciousness reached out to me at a critical time, and his reading of the earlier drafts of this essay sparked new thinking for me and encouraged me to make improvements. John, Terry, and Richard have given so much of their spirits to all of us working in land conservation, and I hope our new directions will encourage them.

My friend and editor, Helen Whybrow, brought this book to life. She heard the stories, read my words, suggested critical reorganizations, and then read my words again. Her great talent and dedication to her craft helped me to find my voice. Helen heard the things that are hard to say and helped bring them into this world. Thank you.

PLEASE GIVE THIS BOOK TO A FRIEND

Gandhi encouraged us to be the change we hope to see in the world. One step in "being the change" is to share the ideas that resonate the most with us. If this essay has struck a chord with you, we urge you to pass it on. Put your name here, leave your scribbles in the margins, and send this book to a friend. Urge others to do the same. Treat this book as a set of ideas, better spread on the winds than left on a shelf.

NAME _____   DATE _____

NAME _____   DATE _____

NAME _____   DATE _____